Cheetah Stories

WriteOn Joliet Cheetah Anthology

By WriteOn Joliet

Cover art by

Mauverneen Blevins

PRINTED IN THE UNITED STATES OF AMERICA
No part of this book may be reproduced or transmitted by any means, mechanical or electronic,
including photocopying, recording, or by any information storage and retrieval system, without
the written consent of the author. For more information, contact
writeonJolietgroup@gmail.com
Cover art by Maureen Blevins
ISBN 9781949777-05-5

www.writeonjoliet.com

WriteOn Joliet cheetah anthology contributors: WriteOn Joliet cheetah anthology contributors: Denise M. Baran-Unland, Mauverneen (Maureen) Blevins, Holly Coop, Diana Estell, Annette Gonzalez, Robert Hafey. Dale Hansen, Jessica Harris, Ryan M. Harris, Tom Hernandez, Todd Hogan, S. Houk, Sue Mydliak, James Pressler, Colleen H Robbins, Jennifer Russ, Stephen T. Saporta, Vanessa JC Stephens

"Well, think about it. I mean, it was still a cheetah, right? A wild animal? We don't allow wild animals in the suburbs."

- *The Strangest Thing* by Tom Hernandez, co-leader, WriteOn Joliet

ABOUT WRITEON JOLIET

WriteOn started as WriteOn Minooka, co-founded by Denise M. Baran-Unland and Kristina Skaggs. Our members come from all over the southern suburbs.

Some have self-published or have been traditionally published. Others are still exploring their writing options and interests. Regardless of our place in the writing world, WriteOn welcomes everyone looking to write, read and grow.

WriteOn Joliet is a welcoming, diverse group of writers of varied skills, interests and experience. The group includes professional journalists, fiction novelists, bloggers, screenwriters, musicians and poets.

We promise a safe, comfortable and supportive atmosphere to share your work, and constructive feedback so that everyone can benefit from our shared knowledge.

WriteOn is a dues-paying organization. The first visit is free.

For more information, visit www.writeonjoliet.com.

TABLE OF CONTENTS

About WriteOn Joliet...5

A Funny Thing Happened on the Way to the Muse by Denise M. Baran Unland...8

A Baby Cheetah Came to my Door and Asked for a Sandwich by Diana Estell...9

A Cheetah Walks into a Bar by Mauverneen Blevins............11

A Guide to Cheetah Etiquette by Jennifer Russ....................14

A Short Cheetah Poem by Maureen Blevins and Vanessa JC Stephens...16

Baby Cheetah by Vanessa JC Stephens..................................17

Edna and the Cat by Ryan M. Harris.....................................19

Finding Your way by Robert Hafey..22

If a Monkey Came to my Door by Holly Coop........................25

Orison by Todd Hogan...27

Revolutionary Whitefish by Annette Gonzalez........................28

Sandwich Lovin' Cheetah by Sue Mydliak...............................31

Seeing Past the Fur by James Pressler....................................34

The Baby Cheetah by Stephen T. Saporta...............................37

The Grilled Cheese Sandwich by Colleen Robbins.................39

The Strangest Thing by Tom Hernandez..................................42

To Distant Shores by Jessica Harris..48

What Kind of Sandwich by Dale Hansen....................................51

Write the Fish by S. Houk...52

Biographies..53

A FUNNY THING HAPPENED ON THE WAY TO THE MUSE

By Denise M. Baran-Unland
Founder and Co-leader of WriteOn Joliet

One day, I received a message from a writer who said coming up with the initial story premise is the hardest part of writing.

In a "Duanne Walton-type" stream of consciousness, and while in the middle of deadlines, I replied:

For me, first drafts are the hardest, crazy because most of my writing is on deadline.

But for fiction, ideas are everywhere.

Some of the most interesting stories are normal occurrences with a "what if" twist.

What if you woke up one morning and looked in the mirror and no one was there?

What if you walked down the street you walked down every day for 20 years and it vanished behind you as you walked?

What if people you were meeting for the first time knew everything about you?

What if a baby cheetah showed up on your doorstep and asked for a sandwich?

This last suggestion sounded so ludicrous, it clung to me. I even suggested this particular writer might wish to write a story based on it. He declined.

Then, my WriteOn Joliet co-leader Tom Hernandez couldn't think of a writing prompt one month. He asked me for one. This anthology is the fruit, er, sandwich of that prompt.

I was so excited to hear what WriteOn Joliet members would write, I forgot to write one of my own. I hope you enjoy these selections at least half as much as I did.

A BABY CHEETAH CAME TO MY DOOR AND ASKED FOR A SANDWICH

By Diana Estell

Cheerio and his mother entered the Free-Range Diner.

"Your usual table, Mrs. Spots?"

"Not today, Chester, I'm signing Cheerio up for the Little Sprinters team. Can he eat here while I'm gone?"

"No problem. Park your rump on the stool, kid."

"Not in public, mom." Squirming, he rubbed his face. Saliva darkened and matted the tan colored fuzz and spots.

"You are never too old for a mother's licks." She headed for the door.

Cheerio climbed onto the stool and looked at the menu on the wall. "Deep fried gazelle gizzards, tangy broiled antelope nestled in wild grass…um…Chester, can you make a shaved wildebeest sandwich?"

"Fresh out. Today's sandwich is grilled warthog."

"With bone marrow chips?"

"Yep and Cola Sludge to drink"

"Yummy, my favorites." Cheerio rubbed his growling stomach.

"Cheezo, marrow it up with wart and sludge," said Chester.

"No prob. Coming up." Cheezo flipped and plated food in a flash.

Cheerio's mouth watered from the smell of fresh meat grilling and sizzling. The diner filled with more customers after he and his mother arrived. Empty tables and stools became extinct.

A baby girl cheetah jumped up and down. A popular rag doll, Fuzzy, flopped and flipped in her hand. Her infant mantle waved along her body as she skipped up to the counter near Cheerio.

"I wan sandywich, I wan sandywich," the girl repeated in a singsong voice." "I wan Jazelle sandywich,"

"There are no more gazelle sandwiches," said Cheerio.

The little cheetah pouted, shouted, stomped and screamed. "I wan sandywich!"

"Shh. Look, Chester's bringing me a grilled warthog sandwich, and it's better than gazelle."

"Momma…I wan momma!"

An adult cheetah came over.

"It's ok Cheery, mommy's right here. We only have to wait a little longer and your aunt will be here. We'll all eat warthog." Her mother picked her up and carried her to their table, Fuzzy flopping over her mother's shoulder.

Cheery smiled, confusing Cheerio.

Cheerio chased the last bites of his sandwich down with Sludge, when…

"Momma look! Jazelle Sandywich is here." Cheery ran into Jazelle's arms. "You're the best, Aunt Jazelle."

"I love you too."

"Not a sandwich, but an aunt?" Cheerio asked Chester.

"Fresh out of uncles. Jazelle's husband is at work. You want to know something funny, kid?"

"What?"

"Their last name is Wart."

"Her name is Jazelle Sandywich Wart?"

"Yep."

Cheerio bent over giggling. His mom came in and paid the bill.

"Did you get enough to eat?" Cheerio's mom asked.

"Yeah, but mom, you won't believe what happened…" His voice lowered as he told his mom about Jazelle Sandywich.

***

A tall, lean, and muscular cheetah came to the counter. "The prices here are high."

"The prices are fairly marked. Good food ain't cheap and cheap food ain't good. If you want, you can go down the street to the Water Buffalo Snack Shack," said Chester.

"They have a catchy jingle."

"Yeah, but the kid's version is better." Chester cleared his throat and began to sing. "Great big gobs of greasy, grimy gopher guts, mutilated monkey meat, little birdies' dirty feet, French fried eyeballs dipped in kerosene, um I forgot my spoon."

The man put a finger on his mouth. "The prices are fine." Gulp. "I'll stay here.

A CHEETAH WALKS INTO A BAR

By Mauverneen (Maureen) Blevins

"A sandwich? You never ask for a sandwich. It's always pie. Pie, pie, pie. What's wrong, Chee?"

"I'm not sure" he said, settling into a booth. "I'm just not feeling myself today."

I brought the sandwich and set it on the table in front of him. He gave it the eye, then yawned and put his chin back on the table.

"You getting enough exercise?" I asked. His eyes didn't seem to have their usual sparkle.

"Yeah. I raced a Gazelle last night. But I just wasn't feeling it. Almost let him win."

"But you didn't?"

"Naaah. After I passed him, I just kept going and went home."

"Everything ok at home? Missus all right?" I asked as I slid into the seat across from him. This wasn't like Chee. His nose twitched as I inched the sandwich a little closer to his side of the table.

"Hippo?" he asked.

His dark eyes were half closed and he seemed focused on something way off in the ether. "I think I'm getting old."

The words were so soft I wasn't sure at first that I'd heard him right, but by the hangdog look on his face, I knew I had. I reached over and put my hand on his paw.

"Aw Chee, you're not old. You beat that Gazelle, didn't you?"

"Yes, but – I didn't CARE."

This was sounding serious. "Maybe you're just bored."

One eye opened and looked right at me. "You're right. I am bored. And those tourists. I am so tired of them not knowing a cheetah from a leopard. Sheesh!"

"Cheeeee? You're not the one who – you know, did in that hunter, are you?"

"Nah. Brit, wasn't he? Too dry. Gotta say he deserved it though."

I couldn't argue. We all felt it was karma. I shuddered. Not much left of that one. Just a few bones next to his show-off pith

11

helmet and big ass rifle.

"I'm thinking of getting a motorcycle." The eye continued to look at me, waiting for my reaction. "But Rita would probably kill me."

Just then the bell on the door jangled, announcing that another customer had walked in. I slid out of the booth to go wait on the zebra and when I looked back to see if Chee was all right, he was gone. So was the sandwich. I smiled. That at least, gave me hope.

The next time I saw Chee was a couple of weeks later. His coat was shiny and his eyes bright as he swaggered in and ordered a couple of pies. To go.

"What kind of pies do you want?"

"You know what my favorite is, but I'll take whatever you got. No wait, make one pigeon."

"For Rita?" I knew her favorite, too.

His grin was something to behold. He nodded and looked out the window. My eyes followed his and widened at the sight of Rita perched on the back of a big black motorcycle.

I looked at Chee, astonished. "She didn't kill you."

"No. We talked, and it turns out she was getting bored too. The kids are gone, and we've got all this time on our hands. We want to see the world."

I found myself tearing up as I put the pies in boxes and put the boxes in a bag with a couple of bottles of water. For the road.

"I'm going to miss you, Chee."

"Aw Deb, I'm gonna miss you too. And your pies. You know you've got the best HippoPIEtomus around." We laughed like a couple of hyenas. I put my arms around his neck, and he nudged a stray tear from my cheek.

I watched through the big window as they eased onto the grassy ruts that passed for a road, Rita perched on the back, the bag with the pies wedged in between them. I kind of envied them. It would be nice to see the world.

I just knew Chee was grinning ear to ear as he laid his ears back and gunned it.

12

Maureen Blevins

A GUIDE TO CHEETAH ETIQUETTE

By Jennifer Russ

It is commonly accepted by the scientific community that the cheetah's favorite meal is a peanut butter, jelly, and potato chip sandwich.

This conclusion, determined through a study conducted by the esteemed Dr. Cletus Pumpernickel, answered the age-old question that plagued and inconvenienced housewives and househusbands for decades:

"My guest is bringing his cheetah over for dinner. Whatever shall I prepare?"

The study, preemptively titled "Don't Freak Out, It's Only a Cheetah" utilized three samples of cheetahs from various social backgrounds and lifestyles. Dr. Pumpernickel specified that all the subjects should be classified as cheetahs or at least have the same number of spots on their bodies. The cheetahs were served various meal combinations including but not limited to roasts, lasagnas, soups, salads, casseroles, and of course sandwiches. Dr. Pumpernickel ultimately ruled out salads after the deaths of three perky but overly-attentive servers.

Months of testing resulted in a thoroughly proven solution to the great cheetah debacle. The following excerpt, taken directly from Dr. Pumpernickel's report, describes in pronounced detail what refreshments must be served in the case of a cheetah surprise.

"In order to please the cheetah, the potato chips must be ridged and of the barbeque variety. The bread should be toasted to just a light shade of brown, close to that of the cheetah's sandy coat, and crust-less to avoid a rather dangerous case of the grumps. Drinks may vary, though plastic cups are highly recommended due to the cheetahs' general lack of thumbs. Cheetahs also have a large and pointed sweet tooth, and they've been known to enjoy cheesecake, tiramisu, and Star Crunch. Those crispy rice puffs bound together with sweet melted chocolate are a sure way to please a cheetah's meticulous pallet. Yum, Star Crunch."

This conclusion freed up a great deal of time spent in grocery stores and took the panic out of millions of eyes when a cheetah inevitably showed up for Christmas dinner. Unfortunately, it did result in the cancellation of the then-popular cooking show, "That's Not a Real Reindeer, It's Made of Styrofoam, Here Eat This Refrigerator Box Instead."

Thanks to Dr. Pumpernickel, we can all rest safely knowing that we have plenty of bread, peanut butter, jelly, and potato chips on hand.

Oh, and don't forget to have a backup toaster. That's how we lost Aunt Ida.

A SHORT CHEETAH POEM

By Mauverneen Blevins and Vanessa JC Stephens

Sweet baby cheetah, why do you come to my door?

I want a sandwich and nothing more.

A sandwich you say? And not just for play.

Do you endeavor to devour all things made of flour or have you come for some meat?

I've come for a treat, be it flour or meat or even a cheese of some kind.

As for the play, perhaps I will stay. I'm sure my mother won't mind.

Oh, I wish we could hang but at the sight of your fang, it may simply be better to say goodbye all together and take your sandwich to go.

If my small cheetah fang does cause you such dread This cat will scat. Thanks for the bread!

BABY CHEETAH

By Vanessa JC Stephens

Off in the distance I hear the thud of someone rapping at my front door. I answer it without hesitation or concern for who it may be.

At first, I see no one until my eyes flitter towards the stoop when I notice the spotted and fluffy baby cheetah.

The tiny speed demon stood fast in its tracks, as startled by me as I was by it. Its large black eyes water in terror at the sight of my gigantic figure looming before it. Each white-ended fiber of its fur dances and glows in the golden light of the setting sun.

I submit to it, kneeling in order to pacify the worried animal.

The cat stalks with slow careful curiosity. As it closes the gap between us, I reached out a jittering hand. It sniffs at the air, then shockingly says "Feed me."

My belly erupts with jarring laughter.

"You talk? How interesting." I say.

"Feed me." It repeats. The words rumble out like a small roar.

"Ha! And what would you like?" I ask. I stroke a hand along his rising back.

"Sandwich." It purrs.

"Any kind in particular?" I chuckle, unable to stifle my wonderment.

The kitty dances around me. Rubbing its head along my back. With my eyes, I try to follow its graceful prance.

"Meat." It demands. Seducing me with its touch.

I roar again with laughter. Such a forceful animal. How can a person say no to something so cute? Standing, I open the screen door and step to the side in order to allow my guest through.

"Come in. I'll make you a fat meat sandwich." My cheeks burn due to relentless smiling.

"Thank you."

The cheetah cub slithers through my legs, entering the home. Quickly, I scan the outdoors. Are there anymore? I close the door behind us.

"I'm about to make a baby cheetah a sandwich." I say though my giggles.

And this is the moment I know the drugs have taken effect.

EDNA AND THE CAT

By Ryan M. Harris

Edna sat at the table in one of the big chairs, so big that her feet couldn't reach the floor and dangled so that they were going numb. She had a small chair father made for her but mother said it didn't match the set and so she had to use a big one. Her arms were crossed, and she glared at the plate in front of her and the raspberry scones she couldn't eat for fear the smallest drop of irreversible red jam might fall on her white Sunday dress and ruin it.

Mother told her that she needed to help them be good hosts, but Edna was having none of it. She didn't believe them about her guest. She didn't believe her mother that he was a Gentleman. She didn't believe her brother who said he'd fought for king and country and distinguished himself against the French at the battle of Nivelle, and she especially didn't believe the maid Cynthia who said he was as charming and handsome as a storybook prince. She didn't even believe her father, whose opinion she trusted in nearly all things, that their guest's unexpected arrival was a surprise inspection from London and that his career might be won or lost during this afternoon's tea.

Edna didn't believe any of this. She was pretty certain their guest was a cheetah.

Their "guest," a large spotted cat weighing well over a hundred pounds sat perched on the chair opposite Edna at the table, its claws digging into and no doubt damaging the fine wood. Its large eyes took in everything in the room. Edna watched his ears. Anytime anyone would move too fast they would flatten against the side of his head. It looked rather funny. He smelled very bad: an intense musky smell that sat heavy in the room and made her eyes water. Her brother Isaac said it was the smell of a predator, and it probably made the French's eyes water as well.

None of this made any sense to her. Why would the King send a cat? How could he hold a sword with paws? You couldn't join the army if you couldn't hold a sword.

"Do you ride?" Her father asked him. Father had been talking about his horses. He'd recently acquired a new trotter from

Derby and was quite proud.

The cat turned to look at father, then continued to turn his head 'til it looked at father sideways but said nothing. He hadn't spoken at all, actually. She could tell it made her parents nervous. Father laughed at the unfunny bits of his own stories when he was nervous, and mother fidgeted.

"Of course, he rides," her brother said. "He's an officer."

"Ah, right, right," Father mumbled.

She poked her brother in the ribs and leaned in to whisper. "Why would he ride a horse? He's a cheetah; they're the fastest animal. I read about them in school they outrun antelope: fifty-five miles an hour or more."

He shushed her and gave her a look like she'd just said the rudest thing.

After tea, they moved to the outside patio where they were served little cups of chocolate mousse. These she was allowed to eat provided she was very careful. Father chose a cigar from a wooden box and offered one to their guest. The cat just sniffed it and then showed no more interest, as he'd turned down everything he'd been offered.

Servant of the King or not, Edna thought he was quite rude.

And, if he was someone so important. Why didn't he have any identification, or have a letter sent ahead on fancy letterhead with the Royal seal? If he was as important as they said he was, he'd have a fancy seal you had to break just to see his real seal which would be even fancier made with real flakes of gold and a silk ribbon that smelled of pineapple, and people who got his letters would know he had so many pineapples he'd make one into juice and soaked ribbons in it just so they would smell nice, and also that he was coming to tea so be ready.

He had only a collar frayed in one corner, on the back of which was printed in simple block letters: Tower of London Mena… It was hard to read after that.

When he had first arrived, father had pondered what the last bit said.

"Tower of London Men at arms," her brother had suggested, and father turned pale.

Father lit his cigar and shook out the match. The smell of cigar smoke soon filled the patio and while it tickled her nose it was a welcome relief from the predator smell her brother found so interesting.

But as the smell drifted on the breeze Edna watched the cat stiffen. His ears went flat against his head and he turned to father wide eyed. His lips pulled back showing teeth.

"EEARRRROARRRRR!" the cat let loose a horrific sound somewhere between a woman shrieking and a dog growling.

"Egad," Father exclaimed, and dropped his cigar.

Her brother moved to cover his ears at the splitting sound and accidently knocked over his cup of mousse. He tried to save it at the last minute and caught the cup but ended up with a glob of chocolate on the knee of his pants.

The cat hissed showing his white teeth.

"Now see here," Father said standing, "I'll not have…"

The cat turned back to father with a look that made father step back. He was a soldier after all, and it was never wise to press a soldier.

The cat gave one last wide-eyed scan of the patio, ears twitching, then bolted. Kicking over the chair he'd been sitting in, he leapt the railing and was in the grass. He cleared their whole yard in quick dash and vanished into the hedge yew. At least fifty miles an hour, Edna thought smugly.

"I'm ruined," Father said sitting back heavily in his chair, cigar smoke roiling up from near his shoe. He laughed and mother fidgeted.

The end.

FINDING YOUR WAY

By Robert Hafey

Tom slowly shuffled down the street while mumbling to himself. April, his wife, had just given him another verbal beating.

"Watching TV is like watching others live your life for you," shouted April. "Since your retirement you have been sitting on your ass in front of that fifty-five-inch flat screen every day," she continued.

Tom took the beating like a man, knowing April was right. Then, thinking he would lighten the conversation Tom shouted back, "Hey, April, I worked my ass off for thirty-seven years," as he stood up, stuck out, and pointed at his rear end.

"You think you're funny - but you're not," April sneered.

Finally, to ease the tension, Tom calmly stated, "I am meeting the guys for a beer. Can I take you out for dinner when I get back?"

Easing up to the escape door while feigning wife deafness, Tom turned the door handle and bounded down the front steps as April droned on and on.

Work had provided structure to his life. Now, he only thought and talked about doing things, but rarely took action. Tom felt lost, but sharing his feelings with anyone, including April, seemed un-manly.

Walking into Moe's Tap immediately relieved the stress he was feeling. Pete, one of his friends, shouted out, "Hey Tommy boy, how are you doing?"

"I am okay," replied Tom, "but April has been on my ass to find something to do other than watch TV."

"Yah, when I retired, Sue and I had the same issues. It takes time to figure things out," chimed in Tony, another friend.

"Hey, I have an idea for you Tom," Pete said excitedly. "You have always been one of the funniest people I know. Did you see the notice about the Open Mic - Comedy Night here at Moe's at the end of the month?"

"No, I did not, and no way could I do that," replied Tom.

Both Pete and Tony immediately shouted out, "Yes, you could - you'd be great."

The talk shifted to other topics, but Tom continued to think about comedy night.

Over dinner, Tom shared the comedy night performance idea with April. She gave him a puzzled, unsupportive look and stated, "But you are not a comedian - why in the world would you want to do that?"

Tom shrugged his shoulders and mumbled, "It was just an idea."

That night when Tom went to bed his mind was spinning. He could not believe how much fun it was laying there in the dark, thinking about all the possible funny stories he could share. For the next two weeks, without telling anyone, he developed, practiced and honed a comedy routine. Then, two days before Open Mic Night, he invited all his friends and April to join him at Moe's for his debut.

The fragrance of fifteen-year-old cigarette smoke and stale beer greeted Tom and April as they entered Moe's. Pushing through the noisy crowd they found an open table up front.

Tom nervously twitched when April asked, "Are you sure you want to do this?"

"Yes," replied Tom firmly, as Pete, Tony and some other friends showed up and joined them.

Everyone else ordered drinks, chatted and enjoyed the early performers, while Tom sat there half-dazed until his name was finally called.

Feeling a slight tingling of paralysis, Tom walked slowly up to the mic. Outwardly he tried to look calm, while inside he felt like his internal organs were shutting down. He took a deep breath, glanced at April and began his routine.

"You know, just the other day, I was sitting on my front porch and a baby cheetah, that's right, a baby cheetah, walked up and asked, "Can I have a sandwich?"

Tom had read all about the importance of comedic timing, so he just let that thought hang out there for at least five to seven seconds.

Then, while scanning the audience and suppressing the urge to laugh he said, "I looked that cheetah right in the eye, and then asked, do you want Cheetos with your sandwich?"

Uncontrollable hoots and hollers filled Moe's to capacity, and then spilled out the front door. The laughter was like a miracle drug. It provided Tom both an intense rush of excitement and a sense of calmness.

Even though every one of his facial muscles wanted desperately to help create a big broad smile, Tom wrestled them to submission in order to maintain his serious comedic face while glancing at April, who was still laughing.

IF A MONKEY CAME TO MY DOOR...

By Holly Coop

I would first ask the monkey's name
And if it was a girl or boy
I'd ask if it could stay for a while
And if the answer was yes
Like a monkey, I would jump for joy

I would invite *Maximilian Monkey* to stay for lunch of course
Calling him *Max,* for short
We would have peanut butter and jelly sandwiches
And for dessert, a decadent chocolate torte
After lunch we'd enjoy some tea
With a little monkeying around in between

Our conversation would be on topics ranging from music to science
Wars to alliance
And we'd question when exactly did the Red Sea part?
And when, from my patio stereo, Mozart began to play
He'd reach to turn the volume - way up
While commenting on the beauty - of my African weaved rug

I would ask intrigued, which are the most annoying bugs?
To how much does a monkey like hugs?
He'd answer by the swatting of a fly
And a flirty wink of his eye

He'd notice while relaxing in my yard
The wonderful tall trees
And the swaying of their green leaves
Under the warm, inviting summer breeze

We would sit and sip lemonade
From plastic cups molded in pineapple shapes
He'd ask do I have an extra pair of shades?

I would oblige by generously handing him
The ones off of my face

After a bit and one last sip he would beg my pardon, as *he* must
now depart

Later that evening when over the fence
Nosey neighbor Gladys would peek
Saying she thought she had seen
A monkey relaxing in my yard

I would shout
Goodness - now
Wouldn't that be bizarre?
Chuckling I would turn to walk in my house
Swatting from my shoulder a menacing, little bug
While entering I'd admire the beauty, of my African weaved rug

When the next week my doorbell rang…
And on the other side stood an orangutan

I simply motioned him in with a shrug
Offered him a cool lemonade
In a pineapple shaped cup

He thanked me with a wink and a hug
While loudly streaming from his ear-buds
I heard playing
The Steve Miller Band's "Jungle Love"

ORISON

By Todd Hogan

Art should be wild, ruthless, and breathtaking.
Creative energy prowls,
    Focusing on a sacrificial subject;
Coiled,
    with feral instincts, inappropriate desires, and unsated hungers
    that have coursed the caverns of imagination for millennia.
Driven to joyful madness,
The artist unleashes a furious pursuit,
Determined to trip up a frenzied, elusive demon
    by using irretractable claws;
Inhaling the dusty heat of an undulating plain,
Taking such powerful strides that
    more than half the time contact with the mundane is lost,
Grasping the pursued by the throat
    to suffocate resistance,
Until burnished, desperate eyes turn opaque
    with final knowledge.
Pausing,
Catching one's breath,
Savoring the heroic, existential struggle that has been waged,
Before devouring
    one more dark enigma,
    successfully overcome.
And so I pray,
Please,
Don't let me be content to write
Like a baby cheetah
On a front porch
Asking for a sandwich.

REVOLUTIONARY WHITEFISH

By Annette Gonzalez

It'd gone 'round 1 am and I was waiting in the dark. It's how we did it.

A light knock on the side door, rap rap…rap…rap. I scurried to the door and opened it slightly. "The chicken is in the pot." I recognized and unlocked. The wood floor creaked, forward, then backward.

"Hello!"

"Good journey, Comrade Cheetah?"

"Yes, but I am hungry. Could you make me a sandwich, or something?"

"Certainly. Whitefish on sesame, OK?"

Nod.

We made our way to the kitchen in the dark. I lit a candle. Prepared the food.

"I have the communique for you. It's in French and Latin, as you requested."

"Good."

"When will you record it?"

"Tonight. But, let's eat first."

"Do you still use that Nigerian coffee?"

"Yes. Njeri still sends it." I smiled.

He nodded.

Comrade Cheetah had always liked whitefish on sesame bagels. It was easy to prepare, and cheap. This time, I'd made the bagels myself.

He'd always been important to the cause. Important to me. But, as of late, he was feeling more his age. His hind legs could not move as quickly as before, the spring in his jumps not as high. I noticed his fur was matted.

He'd been recruited 30 years ago as a young cub. He was strong, virile, completely committed to the cause. His younger years had seen things that no youngster should see. He'd hid in the caves. We found him, cold and hungry. He told us what happened,

28

what he'd seen. We told him of our cause, how we were fighting, but that our numbers were low.

"Can I come with you?"

"Yes, but it won't be easy."

"You look tired."

"I am. It was a long journey from Stalingrad. The safe houses were fewer and farther between this time, and these young people…I don't think they take things as seriously as we do. It's almost like they just want to annoy their bourgeois parents. A rebellion of nothing."

"Armchair anarchy." I chortled.

He laughed.

We finished our food and coffee and he gave me the communique. I read it over, silently. Over the rim of my glasses, I could see he'd fallen asleep in his chair. I woke him gently and motioned him to the small bedroom at the end of the hall. A closet, really, but he liked it.

As I prepared to record the communique, hoping my French and Latin were still up to par, I noticed that everything around me suddenly felt wrong. The table Comrade Yana had made from strong wood planks was now creaky, old, wood splitting. The kitchen items seemed haggard and weary. In the candlelight the tears in the curtains seemed like wicked fingers reaching, groaning silently toward nothing. Pieces of furniture like skeletal remains of the importance we wore like some sort of scapular. Dirty wallpaper holding in the words we held so dear.

We'd known each other for a long time. He was my friend. My comrade. Someone I trusted.

And, we'd been here so many times. In this same house, but this time was different, somehow.

I recorded the Latin version first, the French second. How it angered my parents that I'd 'thrown it all away,' to become a revolutionary. To live in poverty, never settling down, writing for our little nothing newspaper that no one ever bought.

"All those years getting a Ph.D., and for what!" They snarled at me.

After recording the communique, I wondered if it had all been for nothing. I could have been an academic, like my parents. It's what they prepared me for. Still, all that talk of Trotsky and

Lenin and Che' 'round the dinner table had to have some effect. I know they wanted me to be the same as they were; socially conscious academics who talked, just talked. Deeds were necessary.

I stopped myself from continuing down that doubtful path and went to check on Comrade Cheetah. I watched as he lay silent beneath the blankets. The blankets looked as old as we felt; torn bits, fraying on the edges, faded.

The candlelight flicked across his face. He was very still, and calm. I'd always liked watching him sleep As I stared at him, I noticed that the blanket did not rise and fall as it used to. I stared a while longer. I knew. In my heart, I knew that the revolution was over.

SANDWICH LOVIN' CHEETAH

By Sue Mydliak

Summer had come and I had planned to take full advantage of it. Chester had been a real pill as of late, so much so, that I would have taken his spatula and smacked his face or whatever presented itself readily available.

I went over to him and said, "Chester, I am taking a vacation. A much-needed vacation."

"Charlese, you can't! Not now, it's summer!"

"You making a burger?" I asked dryly.

"Yeah, but that has nothing to do with you leaving!"

"It may not, but whoever ordered that might…you're burning it."

"I'm what? Oh, hell, dang it all! See, that's why you can't leave!"

"Chester I can't help it if you can't cook, but I need to get away from this place and you."

A complete look of shock formed on his face. "Me? I didn't do anything to you! Name me one thing Charlese, one thing!"

He thought he had me now. That little glint in his eye told me so. Yeah, well, he's got another thing coming.

I took a deep breath, looked him straight in the eye and said, "I don't do anything right. I'm slow. The customers complain about my so-called bedside manners. I mix the orders up AND you can't read my writing on the tickets."

"Well, yeah! See, you need to stay put and get more practice in!"

I saw red. "Chester Bertie I've been here since the day you opened! I don't NEED more practice! But you're gonna need some. Uh huh, that's right, because you're about to lose a limb and I won't say what one!"

That shocked the socks off him, it did. He was all soppy looking and pleading with them puppy dog eyes. Dang, I wanted to lose myself right there, but I held back. That's when I undid my apron and walked right out.

***

There I was, cool as a cucumber out in my backyard and soaking up some sun. I had died and gone to heaven. Blissful it was. Tammy Wynette was singing *Stand by Your Man.*

Sometimes it's hard to be a woman…

"You got that right girlfriend!"

Giving all your love to just one man…You'll have bad times…

"Damn, straight you will, like now!"

And he'll have good times…

"Why can't I have the good times huh? What's up with that one Tammy?"

Doin' things you don't understand…

"Oh, my God you are so right!"

But if you love him, you'll forgive him…

"Maybe."

Even though he's hard to understand…

"He is! Oh, sweet Jesus, he is!"

But if you love him, oh be proud of him, 'cause after all he's just a man…

"Dumb one at that."

Stand by your man. . .

"Oh, hell, I can't take this anymore I need something more cheerful to make me forget MY MAN."

I took another sip of my special lemonade when I heard it. That screechy voice…

"Charlese! Look what I got."

I turned to look and nearly ran into the house. She had a damn cheetah.

"Ah, Willodean, hunny, watcha got there?" Now, I knew what she had, I was worried that she didn't know.

"It's my dog Rover and look, he's got spots just like a Dalmatian. He's got funny colored fur, I think whoever had him dyed his fur yellow/orange. Should I bleach him back to white?"

"NO! I mean, no. That wouldn't be such a good idea."

"You want to pet him?" she said, coming closer.

I raised my hand up so fast, you'd thought Hitler has just come by.

"No, no, that's alright, but what I do want to ask you is, how did you come by to purchasing — Rover?"

32

"He came to my door and asked for a sandwich."

I — how does one respond to that? I mean . . . wait . . .

"A sandwich? In plain English, he asked for a S.A.N.D.W.I.C.H?"

"Well, sort of, but I knew that's what he wanted, so I made him a cheese sandwich, plain."

I had to do it, I had to say it before I lost all my sanity.

"THAT'S A CHEETAH! Not a dog, not Rover, but a wildcat. See its paws? Do they look like a dog's paw to you?"

"Well, now that you mention it, they do look different."

"THAT'S BECAUSE IT IS DIFFERENT!"

Then reality hit, hard.

"OMG, Charlese! What am I gonna do? What am I gonna do?"

"Well, I don't know, but you can't keep it! It's illegal!"

"I don't want to go to jail! I'm a good girl. I don't want to be somebody's plaything. Help me!"

Plaything? *"Plaything?"*

"Willodean, just call animal control or the zoo and let them know you have a cheetah and they'll come and pick it up."

She and Rover went back to her house and I had enough sun for one day. Later on, Willodean came back over told me that they authorities had come and picked up the cheetah and then went on to say that she made him some more sandwiches for the ride.

SEEING PAST THE FUR

By James Pressler

I hate knocks on the door at seven in the morning. I really hate them on the weekend. And I really, really hate those uninvited guests that feel sunrise is the best time to knock on strangers' doors. I was just grumpy enough to respond to the knocking and give this person a piece of my mind.

Sometimes we get caught off guard even when we are ready for anything. Like when I opened the door to see a young cheetah on my doormat.

"Hello, sir," the cheetah said in a polite tone. "Sorry to disturb you so early in the morning, but could I bother you for some food?"

I thought I was ready for anything. In my defense, I did not know this situation was possible, much less probable.

"You want…food?"

"Uh, yes, if you could be so kind."

Like most people, I don't think straight until my first cup of coffee, and it had just started brewing. Still, I had my doubts about this cheetah on my porch. My grumpy, coffee-deprived, morning mind knew a few basic facts:

Cheetahs were not socially engaging with other predators, particularly humans. Also, cheetahs were native to tropical Africa and not the Chicago collar counties. And of course, the talking thing. Cheetahs can't talk, and here he was, asking for food. Without even a trace of an accent.

My tired mind put together the simplest of strategies – find out what he really was. "Are you really a cheetah?"

The young creature looked over himself, holding out his legs and showing off the spots. "Do I not look like a cheetah?"

"Well, yes." I couldn't think of a brilliant response, so I took the easy route. "Maybe you're just wearing a cheetah outfit."

"Sir," he answered with a feline chuckle, "I assure you that this skin is firmly attached to me, and all the fur is of my own making. Now about the matter of food…"

"Wait." Proving something wasn't a cheetah was more

difficult than it sounded, so I took the alternate route. "Can you prove to me that you're a cheetah?"

"Prove?"

"Yeah. Prove it. Do something special. Do a trick or something that only a cheetah can do."

"Okay." The cheetah brought out a poker deck and fanned it before me in his paw. "Pick a card, any card."

"No," I said, rubbing my face in exasperation. "I mean something I would know a cheetah could do."

He put away the cards. "Sir, I have literally done what no other cheetah could do – I have told you in person that I am a cheetah. Normally you would just have to trust that something was a cheetah without taking their word for it. I offer you my word as a cheetah that I am a cheetah."

"That's not what... what I meant was..." This was going nowhere, so I went for the obvious. "Okay, then how can you talk? I know for a fact that cheetahs can't talk."

The cheetah smiled a bright, feline smile. "You realize that you are saying to the face of a talking cheetah that cheetahs can't talk, right?"

"But that means you aren't what you say you are. If you can talk, that means you can't be anything else other than... well, you can't be a cheetah."

The cheetah drew in a deep breath, and I could tell his response would be a long one. "So, sir, you seem to have this predefined concept of what a cheetah is. You seem to know what my kind does, how we relate to each other, what we are about. These, my friend, are stereotypes. They are simplistic portrayals of the very complex sociocultural structure of my kind. If I may ask, have you ever gotten to know any cheetahs other than, maybe, the zoo?"

I felt embarrassed at his observations and turned away from his gaze. "Uh, some of my friends are cheetahs..."

"Oh, really," he replied. For a cat that shouldn't even be able to talk, I could hear sarcasm in his voice.

"Okay. No. I don't have any friends that are cheetahs. But...I guess I'm just more comfortable around...humans."

The cheetah nodded. "It's always easier to be among your own and just assume things about the world around you, isn't it?"

I bowed my head sheepishly. "Yes."

"Well, maybe this is your chance to learn about us beyond the narrow views of the stereotypes presented by all those groups who just want my kind to be seen as animals. Maybe this is a great opportunity for us to sit down and learn about each other, not as a human and a cheetah, but just as us two individuals, enjoying some breakfast." He sniffed the air. "Do I smell coffee?"

Every point he made struck an assuring chord. "Come on in," I offered. He smiled and entered, wiping his paws politely on the doormat before entering.

We had a delightful breakfast of bagels and coffee that morning. He taught me the card trick he tried to show me – it's actually even more impressive since he performed it with paws rather than hands. And over a plate of bacon, we broke down some stereotypes.

First, his name was Steve. He had been raised in Tanzania but came to the U.S. to seek a career in the theater. He figured there were not many performing cheetahs in plays these days, so it was a ready niche to fill. However, all the presumptions about him being nothing more than a feline meant he did not get many auditions. He lived near the forest preserve and spent his time as an Uber driver as he tried time and again to break into show biz.

However, I also learned about myself. I learned that when my beliefs conflicted with what I saw before my eyes, it might be time to change my beliefs. New ideas and beliefs help us break from the comforting numbness of stereotypes, from the bliss of ignorance that spares us from ever changing our mind. And in doing so, I made a new friend in Steve, and I now have an Uber driver on call at a moment's notice.

But I learned that one stereotype about cheetahs is true from the first ride I got from Steve. Cheetahs are fast.

THE BABY CHEETAH

By Stephen T. Saporta (No claim is made to the work of Ogden Nash)

A baby cheetah came to my door, looking for something to eat;

I know this because, the cat moved its jaws, and miraculously started to speak.

"My coalition of brothers, like so many others, didn't stop me when I started to stray;

"So now here I am, looking for food, in fact I've been looking all day.

"I wandered off from the rest, but when put to the test, the hunter in me was found wanting.

"What I wouldn't give now, for a quick bite of chow; my hunger, I fear, just keeps mounting."

After some hesitation, and with much trepidation, I let the animal into our house.

It leapt onto our couch, then ascended the drapes, when into the room walked my spouse.

"What's going on here?" my wife demanded to know, a look of disdain on her face.

"This cat wanted food, so I let the thing in, not thinking he'd tear up the place."

The cheetah jumped down and started to crawl, its shoulders hugging the ground;

Its haunches were rolling, with each step it took, toward my wife, as it made not a sound.

"Now this thing's stalking me?" My lovely wife cried, as the cheetah slowly drew nigh,

It sprung from the floor, all four feet in the air, its teeth sinking into her thigh;

The claws followed next, wrapping tight all around, my wife's leg beginning to bleed;

"I'm not a bad hunter, after all, am I?" asked the cheetah, as it started to feed.

My dear wife passed out from the shock, from the pain, from the blood and the crushing of bone;

I was left with no choice but to turn and to run and to leave hunter and prey all alone.

As I ran from the scene, as if in a dream, I recalled a short poem from my youth;

My wife's very flesh this cheetah's teeth gnashed, and while Ogden might find me uncouth,

I believe this sad tale must end with a moral, or perhaps with another poem appended;

A cheetah, it seems, is much like a panther, who ought to be feared and respected:

The panther is like a leopard,
Except it hasn't been peppered,
Should you behold a panther crouch,
Prepare to say Ouch.
Better yet, if called by a panther,
Don't anther. (Ogden Nash)

THE GRILLED CHEESE SANDWICH

By Colleen H. Robbins

Joe and I had just closed up the shop after lunch when we heard the tapping on the door. I glanced over the counter as I scrubbed up a stain. The clear glass of the door framed an empty street.

Joe busied himself wrapping the last of the Groundhog Day salads.

I shook my head and continued wiping. A second timid knock sounded. I tossed my rag into the sink and walked over.

There, barely visible above the kickplate, sat a tiny, fuzzy kitten in the snow. A light golden brown in color, slightly darker stripes and spots marked its sides. Very, very cute, if a bit bedraggled. It opened up incredibly wide eyes and looked up at me.

I couldn't resist. I opened the door and scooped up the kitten, then closed and locked the door again before anyone could slip inside.

"Traci, what are you doing?" Joe shook his head slowly. "Don't bring that dirty little cat in here. Put some water out back for it. If the Health Department sees it, they'll shut us down in a heartbeat."

"I'd prefer a grilled cheese sandwich." A tiny voice, no bigger than the kitten. "On white bread, with mayonnaise and bacon, please. And a thick slice of spam." It licked its foot. "And lots of butter on the bread."

"It talks!" Joe grabbed a broom and held it like a baseball bat.

"Ow!" I dropped the kitten as I scrambled out of the way. The kitten sank needle-sharp kitten claws into the legs of my jeans to stop its fall. Claws about three times longer than those of a normal kitten. Blood slowly oozed out, staining my jeans. "C'mon, let go."

"Don't drop me again." It slowly released my legs. "Can I have my sandwich now?"

Joe leaned over. "A little kitten like you should not be eating all that garbage."

"But I'm very, very hungry."

"We don't even have most of those ingredients," I explained. The kitten looked up at me, tail stiffening. "No bacon, no spam, no cheese, no butter, no mayonnaise, and no white bread. Poof! No sandwich."

The kitten looked back and forth between Joe and I, then over at the prep counter. "You have bread over there."

"Flat bread, made with no milk or eggs."

"Well, what's that white stuff?"

"Tofu." I sliced off two thin pieces and laid them on a piece of flatbread. I added a slice of beefsteak tomato, a wide swath of hummus, and topped it off with red bean curd. "We're a vegan shop."

"Can't you at least put some vegan sour cream on it?"

I looked down at the kitten. "No, sweetie, there's no such thing as vegan sour cream."

"Is it vegan if it comes from organic cows?" The kitten shook its head. "How can you tell if a cow is organic, anyway?"

"It doesn't matter. Vegans don't eat or use anything that came from animals."

"But it doesn't hurt the cow to give milk."

"It might hurt her calf that should have been drinking the milk."

The kitten looked ready to cry. "Very well, do your best."

When I put the sandwich plate on the floor, the kitten eyed it warily before nibbling at the tofu. "This isn't too bad, actually."

A moment later the kitten dove into the plate. In minutes, the food vanished, and the kitten's belly swelled almost too much to walk.

"Thank you, thank you. I'll be on my way. I'll come back next year for another sandwich."

***

When Groundhog Day came around again a year later, we made another "grilled cheese" for the kitten.

"Do you think it will come back? It's probably all grown up. Maybe we should make two."

Joe finished putting the last spoonful of red bean curd on the second sandwich when the kitten arrived and tapped on the door. "I've come for my sandwich."

His rosette-spotted fur was thicker, claws longer, and teeth sharper. Neither Joe nor I reached to unlock the door.

We really hadn't expected a cheetah.

THE STRANGEST THING

By Tom Hernandez

I slurped another gurgle of beer and tipped the frosted mug toward my friend, Chuck, perched on the next stool.

"Yeah, so the strangest thing happened to me the other day."

"Do tell."

"I was watching the Sox game – they were losing again, what a shitty season they're having this year!"

"Ok, nothing too strange about that."

"Hold on, I'm not finished. I was watching the game when I heard someone knocking on the door."

I raised the glass to my lips once again. It was a hot day. I was parched and couldn't get the cold, amber relief to the back of my throat fast enough.

"And?"

"Hold on Mr. Impatient! So, I got up and answered the door, and what do you think I saw there?"

"Jeezus, man, I don't know! Please just tell me. I have to get home some time tonight or my wife is going to kick my ass. I've been out every night this week."

Chuck sipped his Crown Royal neat, his drink of choice ever since we met in college thirty years ago. He tossed a handful of corn nuts into his mouth just as I started to answer. Bad timing on my part.

"It was a baby cheetah – Hey! Don't choke!"

I firmly smacked Chuck on the back to help him find his breath.

"What the hell? Did you say a baby cheetah?"

"Yep."

"A baby cheetah? As in, a jungle cat?"

"Technically they live more on the plains of Africa, but yes."

"Ah, yes…I should have known that factoid," he said, a little too dry and snarky for my taste.

Still, he is my best friend, so I let it go. He took another drink to try to wash down the rogue corn nut remnants. "Ok wise guy, what gives? And get to getting to the point already…"

"So, like I said…"

"Hold on one doggone minute!" Chuck pushed his left palm nearly into my face. "Just stop right there. Is this another one of your stupid long-winded jokes?"

"Sir, I do not know to what jokes you refer." I elevated my nose slightly, feigning indignation at his disdain and doubt-ridden suggestion.

"You know what the hell I mean. I mean like the one about a moth flying into a podiatrist's office that goes on and on and on forever before you finally get to the stupid punchline and laugh yourself silly."

"Tsk-tsk…" I clicked my tongue loudly and rolled my eyes. "Don't take it out on me just because you have no taste or sense of humor."

"I have no sense of humor? Mr. Kettle, may I introduce you to Mr. Pot?"

"Whatever. You mock, but I swear, this is absolutely true. So, there I was, staring down at a baby cheetah. And guess what happened next?"

"Here we go again…" Chuck turned away and grabbed another handful of nuts.

"The cheetah asked for a sandwich."

A storm of half-chewed, spit-cemented nuts spewed from Chuck's mouth. I kind of felt bad for the guy. He is my best friend, after all. Well, maybe not all that bad, but a little sympathetic, at least.

"Hardy-har-har," Chuck said, slamming into each syllable. "He talked? A baby cheetah talked to you? He used actual words?"

"Naturally. How else do you think he asked for a sandwich? Sign language?"

"Fine, Mr. Smarty Pants. I'll bite. So what kind of a sandwich did he request? Antelope? Gazelle? Hippo?"

"Of course not! That's just stupid. First, why would I have any of that? And second, it's a baby cheetah. Haven't you heard a word I've said? It wanted peanut butter and jelly, like all kids."

"Ok, if you say so."

"I know so."

"Fine. So, when this cheetah…"

"Baby cheetah."

"Right. Baby cheetah. When this baby cheetah magically shows up on your porch…"

"Uh-huh."

"…and speaks to you…"

"Now you've got it."

"In English, no less…"

"Why wouldn't it speak English? This is America, after all."

"…and asks you for a peanut butter and jelly sandwich…"

"Uh-huh."

"…what did you do?"

"What anyone would do. I went back in the house and made a peanut butter and jelly sandwich."

"And you served it to him – I'm sorry, I'm assuming it was a male?"

"Good question. Truthfully, it was hard to tell. I was so amazed that words were coming from his mouth that I didn't really look at its hind quarters, if you know what I mean. Plus, you know, at that age, the male voice sounds just like a girl's so I can't say for sure."

"Ah, of course," Chuck said, letting this tidbit of clean, clear, pure logic roll over his brain. "Silly me! What am I thinking? So, you served the sandwich to it?"

"Certainly! Why wouldn't I? Poor, little thing looked hungry, and it'd come all that way from…wherever it came from. But first I invited it in. I didn't want to be rude."

"Heaven forbid! So, what did you do then?"

"What any reasonable person would do. I offered him a side to go with his sandwich."

"Let me guess – Cheetos?"

I waved my index finger at Chuck in agreement. "Aha! You would think so, right? But no, he said he doesn't like the orange dust rubbing off onto his fur. So, I gave him goldfish crackers to go along with the sandwich…"

"Goldfish crackers?"

"Again, kids love the goldfish. Don't you know anything about anything? Plus, you know, a cheetah? Cat? Fish?"

"Ah! Of course! Shame on me for not connecting such obvious dots and appreciating your magnificent thoughtfulness. Then what?"

"I gave him a glass of milk."

"I get it now – cats like milk," Chuck said, triumphantly.

I looked at Chuck like he had two heads on his shoulders. "How the hell should I know what cats like? You know perfectly well that I have two dogs and a parakeet. I am allergic to cats. How long have you known me? And you call yourself my best friend?" I rose from the barstool as if to leave.

Chuck grabbed my shoulder and shoved me back onto the stool. "Sit back down, you idiot, and finish telling your incredible story."

I smiled, happy with my small victory. I didn't win many such battles with Chuck. Taller, more attractive, quick witted, a naturally gifted musician, he'd also always been wiser and cleverer than me. I love him like a brother – maybe even more than my own brothers, truth be told – but I admit, envy sometimes rears its ugly green head when it comes to my best buddy. So, every win, no matter how miniscule, was to be celebrated.

"Well, Ok. That is, only if you really want to hear it."

"Yes. Pretty please, Freddie. Please honor me with the rest of your story," Chuck said, stretching and dragging each word for melodramatic emphasis.

"Ok, so, where was I?"

"You'd given the mysterious talking baby cheetah a peanut butter and jelly sandwich and goldfish crackers because that's what children like, and a glass of milk because…You didn't say why you gave it a glass of milk."

"Because milk goes perfectly with peanut butter, of course!"

"Of course. Why didn't I think of that? So, then what did you do?"

"Well, we talked for a while."

"About?"

"You know, the usual. The weather, politics, sports. He's a big football fan. Likes the Bears, but his favorite teams are the Detroit Lions and the Carolina Panthers."

"Go figure!" Heavy laughter finally rolled through the new smile on Chuck's face. "So, then what?"

"Then I politely excused myself, went back to the kitchen and out to the garage."

"Why did you go to the garage, pray tell?"

"Because I keep my guns in a locked cabinet in the garage, so our kids can't get at them."

"Wha...?" I had Chuck right where I wanted him, stuck in a briar patch of befuddlement.

"I took my revolver from the cabinet, marched back into the house and shot the cheetah right where he sat – oops, sorry, I mean, it."

Chuck's eyelids and mouth rattled open like broken window shades. "What the hell? You shot and killed a talking baby cheetah that had come to your door and asked for a sandwich? Are you insane? Why would you do such a thing?"

"Well, think about it. I mean, it was still a cheetah, right? A wild animal? We don't allow wild animals in the suburbs. He could have grown up to kill us all. Or at least eat our pets!" Every muscle in my cheeks, forehead, eyebrows and chin strained under the immense pressure to hold back a guffaw. God, I was enjoying this.

His face now an ice sculpture of confusion, he slowly shook his head. "But...wha...that doesn't make any...I mean...How..." Words spluttered through his lips like water through a clogged faucet.

Straight-faced, I continued. "Don't worry about it! Everything is fine! I cleaned the fur real nice. No blood stains at all. Then I skinned it and cooked the meat. You ever had baby cheetah?"

No reply.

"Tastes just like ham. A little less salty, but good."

Still no response. I could barely contain my glee. I prepared my final salvo. Took a deep breath. Then fired.

"Speaking of ham, did I ever tell you about the time I went to see Bob Franco, who lives on a farm?"

46

Finally, Chuck looked at me through eyes still glazed with the image of me eating a talking baby cheetah. "What? Who? Bob? The guy we knew from our freshman math class in college?"

"Yep. The very same. He's a farmer now, and when I pulled up to his house, I noticed this three-legged pig kind of hip-hopping around the side yard. So, I asked Bob, 'Hey, why does that pig have only three legs'?"

Chuck stared at me for about fifteen seconds. I tell you, if his eyes could have shot lasers, I'd have been a pile of ash. Finally, he spun off the bar stool, grabbed a handful of corn nuts and whipped them at my head. He stampeded toward the bar's front door, nearly toppling a waitress carrying a tray of drinks.

"Chuck! Wait!" I gasped through pounding waves of laughter.

Skating across the floor in five long steps without so much as a "good bye," he slammed the door just as the words escaped my lips. He didn't hear them, but I didn't care. I had finally gotten his goat – or, cheetah, as it were.

I held my sides to keep from keeling over with laughter and yelled into the beer-battered barroom air.

"Chuck! Come back! Don't you want to know why this pig has only three legs, Chuck? It's the strangest thing!"

TO DISTANT SHORES

By Jessica Harris

He had just sat down to dinner; a simple meal of fish he didn't sell and chips he made from potatoes in his garden. The night was pleasant with a salty breeze blowing in and the quieting cry of sea birds. It was interrupted by a knock on the door. Between the table and door, the knocking increased in pitch and frantic desperation.

Past the rusty swing and creaking groan of wood, the fisherman was surprised to see a little boy there, hand still poised to knock. He stared at the scruffy fisherman with wide eyes for several moments, almost as if embarrassed to be caught. The fisherman had been expecting some company, but they usually came in waves. He poked his head out and looked left and right for signs of anyone else. He looked to make sure his porch light was on: a beacon to his guests. It was.

He returned his attention to the little boy. He wore a once-bright yellow raincoat spotted in mud, making the fisherman instantly think of a baby cheetah, and equally awkward rain boots. His sandy hair was plastered to his head, and his eyes stared at him in wonderment.

"I need a sammich," the boy said.

"What was that?" The fisherman asked.

"I need a sammich," he said again, this time more adamantly. After a moment, the fisherman was able to deduce by "sammich" the boy meant "sandwich."

"Of course, come in."

The boy launched into the house. His squeals of delight echoed off the walls that hadn't heard laughter since Martha died – but no, perhaps it was better not to think on that. The fisherman made himself busy in the kitchen, putting together a peanut butter and jam sandwich; his favorite when he was a boy. He cut two thick slices of dark bread and slathered them both to make any boy's delight. His heart soared as he heard the child's enthusiastic playing: tangling himself in the fishing nets, jumping with muddy boots on the bed, zipping from wall to wall.

The fisherman set the plate down and called to the child, who launched himself on the bench and set upon the meal with a relish.

"What is your name, boy?" he asked.

"Fromus," the boy said with his mouth full.

"Thomas?" the boy nodded and continued to happily munch. The fisherman watched the boy carefully, his own meal forgotten. Something odd struck him about the boy and with realization born of experience, he knew what it was.

"Say, Thomas, are you sure you were to come to me asking for a sandwich?" The boy nodded, oblivious to the leading question. "There's nothing else you needed to ask me for?" The boy shook his head. The fisherman tried to think of a way to get the boy to answer. "Nothing at all?"

"Nuh-uh," the boy said. "I had to come to the fisherman and ask for a sammich," he said.

"I see. Could it possibly have been something that sounds like 'sammich'?" The boy's chewing slowed, and the fisherman watched as he appeared lost in a deep thought. "Could you have been sent here to ask for the 'ghost ship'?" The boy grew quiet then, picking at his coat. "Thomas? I need to hear you ask me, son."

"Can I have...the ghos'hip?" he muttered.

"Clearly now, boy. Speak up."

"I need the ghost ship," he said again. When he looked up his eyes were panicked. He nodded once more and reached a grubby hand to the fisherman, who took it.

"Okay." He smiled warmly at the boy. "Don't worry, you have nothing to be afraid of."

He got up from the table and drew around him a deep-cowl cloak and put on a conical hat to protect him from the cold of the sea breeze. Around his neck he carried a scythe-shaped pendant that had been a gift from a farmer. He shut off his porch light and took the boy's hand.

They walked down the beach, past the docks mooring fishing vessels to a rocky outcropping that jutted into the sea. The fisherman walked boldly on a hardly seen path while the boy never questioned his guide. It led to a quiet and secluded cove in which was docked a mysterious boat. The fisherman undid the rope and tossed it on board while the boy played. This ship was different from the others; it contained no motor, no riggings. It was a simple wooden structure propelled by oars and manpower. Otherwise there was a single bell, turned green from salt and sea.

Once man and boy were secured, he began to row. The boy kept himself occupied by playing with whatever he could find, his childhood enthusiasm brimming again after his earlier forgotten melancholy. He giddily reached for the bell.

"Careful, boy!" The fisherman exclaimed, causing the child to freeze. "That must be handled with great care." The reprimand startled Thomas, who sat down instantly in mute obedience. The fisherman sighed, feeling guilty. "Would you like to ring the bell?" He asked after a moment.

"Yessir."

"You can but be careful." The boy grinned as he reached for the chain. Just like always, a somber stance enveloped the boy as he held it and it was several minutes of only ocean waves and sea breeze.

Dong! Dong! A moment of silence. Then another. Dong!

The funerary dirge begun.

The sun arose on that secret cove to see a mysterious, old fashioned boat docked. It was empty, though the swells and falls from the waves left it calmly rocking, silent to the number of trips it made that night. Down the length of the beach, people stirred; mostly fisherman, among them an old man alone who left the remains of a half-eaten sandwich on his table. Porch lights dimmed and darkened as they began their day. The sun rose red on the horizon.

Red sun at night, sailors delight. Red sun in the morning, sailors take warning.

WHAT KIND OF SANDWICH

By Dale Hansen

A baby cheetah came to my door,
and asked me for a sandwich.

I asked him to come in and said,
You may very soon be dead.
As fastest as you can run,
You may be too very slow.

You have had trouble with humans,
We have destroyed your habitats.
From poaching you will lose,
From your numbers you will lose.

I'm sad that you may not survive,
So come on in and remain alive.
Stay a while with me in my house,
Have a sandwich with my Cheetos.

WRITE THE FISH

By S. Houk

I never like it when I see poetry smack in the middle of a page in a novel or a story. It takes me out of it. It stops the flow. My mind was far away in the heart of a brave child or in the breast pocket of a woman with an amulet – pink and fragrant with old spices – drawing a lover to her.

Which lover? It's so problematic. Good lovers don't make it to the page. Ink is only spilled across the footfalls of idiotic lovers – the ones who can't allow themselves to be happy. I'm not interested in the lovers who through goodness or patriotism suffer. No. Give me the ones who ruin their lives with fear and sheer stupidity. Error, especially if boldly made, is the stuff of writing.

Whoever chiseled, "Odin is kind and remembered my birthday"? No one. We chisel, "He was complicated and conflicted. A stupid force of nature I had to possess. It ruined me. I'd do it again." You don't write the water. You write the fish.

Or, in the case of fits of fancy, you write the cheetah. If I were a baby cheetah knocking on a door, I might say I wanted a sandwich, but that would be a lie. I would want more of what I already have – speed. I would wander around your house like a vampire looking for the *Flash* superpower that is resident in your forgotten belongings, sequestered in your veins, quivering in your desires. And I will take it. Call me Odin. I won't give any of it back. I'll be a force of nature you can possess for a while. I'll ruin you – and you would do it again. The price to be paid for being eaten by a cheetah: immortality.

> what say you sailors
> water in your mouths
> black below
> blue above
> a bubbly surrender

BIOGRAPHIES

Denise M. Baran-Unland is the author of the Bryony Series supernatural/literary trilogy for young and new adults, the Adventures of Cornell Dyer chapter book series for grade school children and the Bertrand the Mouse series for young children.

Baran-Unland has six adult children, three adult stepchildren, fourteen total grandchildren, six godchildren, and four cats.

She is the co-founder of WriteOn Joliet and previously taught features writing for a homeschool co-op, with the students' work published in the co-op magazine and The Herald-News in Joliet.

Baran-Unland blogs daily and is currently the features editor at The Herald-News. To read her feature stories, visit www.theherald-news.com.

To buy her books, read her blog, and follow her on social media, visit www.bryonyseries.com.

Mauverneen (Maureen) Blevins is a writer/photographer who has spent most of her life in the Joliet area.

She has been published in newspapers and anthologies that range from the Chicago Tribune to the "Cup of Comfort" series. She currently edits a classic car magazine called The Dashboard for which she also writes and does the photography.

Two blogs also keep her busy writing. Positively Tuesday is an attempt to foster a little less negativity in our lives and Mauve On The Move is a travel blog, highlighted by her award-winning photography – her other passion.

She has three grown daughters and now has a four-legged companion named Bailey.

For more information and to read her blogs, visit www.mauveonthemove.com and maureenblevins.blogspot.com.

Holly Coop resides in Joliet with her family. She is an author and artist. She enjoys writing spiritual and inspirational poetry and motivational quotes.

Coop has self-published three books, *A Cup of Inspiration To Go Please – My Heart Runneth Over*, *Heart Strings – Forever Wander*, and *Locks of Love – A Book of Encouragement.*

She also publishes a blog, writerbeeme.blogspot.com, and has an Etsy shop, hollycoopcards.etsy.com. Purchase Coop's books at HollyCoopBooks.com.

Diana Estell: The joy and pains of Estell's personal story, as well as her educational background, have shaped her writing style.

Estell has a Bachelor of Arts from Northern Illinois University and it was there, while writing for her classes in anthropology, that her love of writing re-awoke.

Growing up, Estell had a book in her hand constantly. Books like Little House on the Prairie, Little Women, and countless others. The love of words is a deep passion of hers.

She enjoyed reading the dictionary, taking words and changing them into new words. Words were her imaginary playground, a veritable lush garden, springing out blossoms of creativity.

When Star Wars blasted into orbit, so too did Diana's love for all things fantasy. Dungeon and Dragons and Star Trek played a significant role in her private imaginary world. Now the worded playground, with its abundant flora, sprung forth thorns of sharpened steel. Planets and creatures emerged with ease. This passion for fantasy never left but has grown stronger.

Estell has traveled extensively, most recently to Paris, France. Her love for history, martial arts and weapons is woven into her writings. She has a black belt in a martial arts blend of Taekwondo and Jujitsu.

She had anticipated she would be going on archeological digs after graduating, but childhood dreams never die. No matter how many layers of her past accumulated, nothing could stop a story from emerging in her mind.

Estell's first novel, *Abyss of the Fallen*, is scheduled for release in 2019 by Brimstone Fiction.

Email her at inklings67@aol.com

Annette Gonzales currently lives in Joliet but spent most of her adult life in the Washington, DC area.

She writes very short stories, sudden fiction, poetry, fiction noir, but her favorite writing format is creative non-fiction.

Annette is the former editor and publisher of *Spiraeas: A Journal of Literature and Art* which was based in Prince George's County, Maryland.

She is a graduate of University of Baltimore's Graduate School of Liberal Arts.

Robert B. Hafey has authored three books.

These are a memoir, *Boomhood – A Baby Boomer's Free-Range Childhood* and two technical books, *Lean Safety – Transforming Your Safety Culture with Lean Management and Lean Safety Gemba Walks – A Methodology for Workforce Engagement* and *Culture Change*.

He currently resides in Homer Glen, Illinois.

Dale Hansen is retired and spends his time reading, running, mentoring others and watching his grandkids.

He enjoys leading small Bible study groups which he has done for over thirty years. Dale has published two Bible devotionals.

He has enjoyed and learned a lot from the WriteOn group. He is married with two married daughters and three grandsons.

He lives in Joliet.

For more information, visit Groundedandgrowingweekly.com.

Jessica Harris was born in Chicago, but she has lived across the United States and Europe and traveled extensively. She attended Trinity Christian College and Oxford University and graduated with a degree in history and education.

After beating cancer, she married Ryan Harris in a castle (made complete with a groom-led archery shoot). She currently lives in Florida with Ryan and their Newfoundland Dublin.

She's written multiple novel-length works and numerous short stories. This is her first publication.

Ryan M. Harris was born in Indiana and has lived all over the United States. In 2017 he married Jessica and the couple currently resides in Florida.

Ryan's education is in philosophy having attended Marion University and IUPUI.

He has been writing seriously for about ten years. He writes mostly short fiction. This is his first anthology publication.

Tom Hernandez is a writer, public speaker, performer and communications professional.

Born and raised in Joliet, Illinois, Tom has been writing personally and professionally since childhood. His writing explores the many complicated facets of life —family, faith, social justice and politics.

He and his wife Kellie have two adult daughters and welcomed their first grandchild in 2018. They live in Plainfield, Illinois.

Tom has published three books: *Chocolate Cows and Purple Cheese and other tales from the homefront* (essays about young adulthood and parenthood), *Abundance* (poetry), and *The Edge of Middle* (essays, poetry and fiction about the trip to middle age).

For more information, visit tomhernandezbooks.com.

Todd Hogan is a writer who grew up in Joliet, Illinois, in a Catholic family of ten kids.

He married his wife, from a family of six kids, at Notre Dame where he graduated. He also graduated law school from the University of Arkansas. He returned to practice law and teach, before working in Chicago in various capacities for a large commercial insurer.

Hogan and his wife have returned to Joliet, living in the same home where she grew up. His published short stories appear in several anthologies.

Sharon M.E. Houk writes mostly poetry and short stories. Favorite themes include knock-down drag-out fights and soaring triumph over one's enemies both mathematical and toothy.

She also writes essays, books, and plays. She paints whenever she can and has been known to attach random objects to canvas considering the result captivating in the way a magpie might eye a pop-top.

Recent collaborations have included a video entitled The Pledge in which the wonderful Tim Shilling and Ingy's Piano Bar of Akron, Ohio created the musical soundtrack. She is also a member of the Irish American Society of County Will, Latitude 41 theatre group, and Romeoville Art Society.

When not writing, Sharon can be found doing IT work, teaching at Lewis University, and walking in the forest. She lives in Joliet with her imaginary Irish wolfhounds.

Follow Houk at sharonhouk.blogspot.com.

Sue Mydliak lives in Illinois with her husband and has been writing for 10 years.

She started writing when the book "Twilight" first came out and fell in love with the paranormal genre.

Since then, she has written and finished her Rosewood Trilogy and just recently her anniversary edition, "Forever," which is the first book re-written for adults.

Currently, she has two books in progress, "Southern Shorts," which is an anthology of short stories about Dry Prong, Louisana and Night Games. Both will be out next year.

For more information and to purchase her books and artwork, visit suemydliak.wordpress.com and fineartamerica.com/profiles/sue-midlock.html.

James Pressler is a career analyst who, for two decades, has lived a double-life as a creative writer.

This simple hobby became a passion for bringing new perspectives to familiar themes, with moods ranging from friendly humor to serious observations.

Along with a dozen short stories and character sketches published over the past several years, James's first novel, *The Book of Cain*, was released in 2018. His next novel, *Small-Town Monster*, is due to be published later this year.

James blogs twice a week about *Writing and "The "Process"* at writingandtheprocess.com.

Colleen H Robbins has been writing since she was nine years old and holds a Bachelor of Arts degree in English Language and Literature from Lewis University.

She has attended numerous workshops, including the Iowa Summer Writer's Conference in 2003, the six-week long Odyssey Fantasy Writer's Workshop in 2007, and TNEO in 2009 and 2013.

Her stories, poems, essays, and articles have appeared under a variety of names in everything from small regional magazines to the gaming-oriented magazines Different Worlds and The Dragon, and has been included in numerous anthologies.

She writes both mainstream (literary) fiction and genre (science fiction, fantasy, and horror), and is the author of the Daraga series. Contact her at shavaya@aol.com.

Jennifer Russ is a freelance writer focusing on animal welfare and human rights.

She is the author of "Whitewallsville: One Man's Journey Through Tigers, Frozen Birds, and Suicide," a story of grief and redemption set within the walls of a mental institution.

When Jennifer is not tackling serious topics, she enjoys petting dogs, smelling old books, cosplay, and traveling the world. She is currently working on a fiction project about the children of Tibet.

Stephen T. Saporta has been an attorney in good standing in Illinois since his admission to the bar in 1987.

Saporta earned his bachelor's degree in Chemistry from Northwestern University (1983) and his Juris Doctorate from Valparaiso University where he distinguished himself as an articles editor for the Valparaiso University Law Review (1986).

He served as a judicial clerk for the Indiana Supreme Court (1989 – 1991) and established Saporta Law Offices the following year. Saporta became a registered patent attorney with the United States Patent and Trademark Office in Alexandria, Virginia (2000), and earned a Master of Laws Degree in intellectual property from John Marshall Law School (2001).

Over course of his career, Saporta has represented clients in a wide variety of practice areas in both state and federal court. He maintains an office in Joliet, Illinois, and has served as the Will

County Member at Large on the board of the Association of Foreclosure Defense Attorneys since 2010. Saporta has successfully defended scores of homeowners who have faced foreclosure in Will, Cook, DuPage, Grundy, Kane, Kendall, LaSalle and Livingston Counties in Illinois.

Saporta's published works include:

- "Tax Shelter Registration: An Alternative Proposal That Leads to the Efficient Identification of Abusive Tax Shelters," VALPARAISO UNIVERSITY LAW REVIEW, Volume 20, Number 3, pp. 489 – 530 (Spring, 1986).

- "Residential Mortgage Foreclosure Defense In Illinois," NATIONAL ACADEMY OF CONTINUING LEGAL EDUCATION (May 16, 2014). Available at: https://www.nacle.com/CLE/Courses/The-Fundamentals-of-Foreclosure-Defense-and-Alternative-Remedies-567

- "To Love is the Greatest!," RACK UP A VICTORY: A "SPECIAL" MANUAL FOR YOUR BILLIARD JOURNEY, STUDENT OF THE GAME... ...AND LIFE!!, pp. 56 – 59 (© 2016 Thomas D. Rossman). Available at: drcue@artisticpool.org

- DIVINE APPOINTMENT (© 2017 Stephen T. Saporta). Available at: WillCountyLawyer@aol.com

Vanessa JC Stephens lives in Joliet, Illinois with her husband and daughter.

Stephens was bitten by the writer's bug when her third-grade teacher gave her a blank hardcover book to fill with words and illustrations for the young authors club, she' been writing in one form or another ever since.

She enjoys writing short stories, screen plays, poetry, and is currently working on her debut gothic fiction novel.

When Stephens is not writing, she can be found with a hook and yarn crocheting afghans for family, friends, and the elderly.

For more information, visit Stephen's blog *Life in the Middle* at vanessajcstephens.com.